THIS BOOK is to

commemorate the issuance of the

official Southern Ute medal

November 15, 1974

and is limited to 15,000 copies

No. *6604*

Leonard C Burch

Photograph by John I. Griffi

THE SOUTHERN UTE have made great strides in their advancement through the ages as shown here; the tepee in the foreground depicts the old way while the marquee for their new motel complex is seen in the background.

THE
SOUTHERN
UTE
PEOPLE

by Robert W. Delaney

Scientific Editor: Henry F. Dobyns
General Editor: John I. Griffin

PUBLISHED BY INDIAN TRIBAL SERIES / PHOENIX

THE SOUTHERN UTES

HEADQUARTERS: Ignacio, Colorado

POPULATION: Utes of the Mouache and Capote bands numbering about 900.

RESERVATION: The boundaries enclose 818,000 acres of land in southwestern Colorado, mainly in the Pine River Valley, but less than one half of that (305,000 acres) is Southern Ute land: 5,291 acres of allotted land and 298,277 acres of tribal land which is held in common.

LANGUAGE: Uto-Aztecan

These are cold statistics and in no way introduce the reader to one of the most progressive tribes of Indians in the United States. Under excellent leadership, the Southern Utes have embarked on a "people" program of social and economic development to prepare their membership for life in this mechanized and modern world. Their tribal organization is very modern to the extent that other Indian groups have used it as a model to develop their own programs and governmental structure. With the initiative of their leadership, the Southern Utes are achieving some of their goals and making inroads on problems yet to be solved.

The statistics, too, do not say that the present-day Southern Ute reservation is a narrow strip of land measuring fifteen miles by seventy-three miles running from the Continental Divide in southern Colorado westward toward the boundary with the Ute Mountain Ute reservation. It is a land that encompasses the stream valleys of the Piedra, Pine, and Animas Rivers and extensive, undulating, semi-arid mesas and mountains in between. This is high, dry country; the elevation varying from a little less than a mile above sea level to 7,500 feet. (The town of Ignacio is 6,424 feet in elevation.) A sparce, scattered growth of juniper and sage is seen on the grayish white mesas throughout most of the reservation with irrigated farms forming occasional patches of green on an otherwise brown landscape. Not all of the land within the reservation is owned by Southern Utes. More non-Indians than Indians live within the boundaries. This has resulted in a "checkerboard" pattern on the reservation and makes it difficult to manage agricultural, timber, and other resources. One tribal member characterized the pattern of the reservation as a "moth-eaten rug".

Finally, the statistics cannot show that the Southern Utes are highly respected by the so-called Anglos and Hispaños who live on the reservation and nearby. Theirs is a tri-ethnic area, fascinating to anyone interested in people and their relationships. Today, as more and more people become involved in discovering the past, many from across the nation come to the Southern Ute reservation to spend their vacations with these Indians, staying in the Pino Nuche Purasa, the very modern tourist complex owned and operated by the Southern Utes.

To these tourists and others, it is hoped that this book will help to tell the story of the Southern Utes: their background, contacts with European cultures, vacillating relations with the United States government, establishment of their current boundaries, and their emergence into a knowledgeable and progressive group of people.

LEONARD C. BURCH
Chairman
Southern Ute Tribal Council

Leonard Burch was born December 24, 1933, and grew up in Ignacio, Colorado. He attended school in his hometown and upon graduating in 1954 joined the United States Air Force.

After four years in the military, young Burch returned to Ignacio and served as realty officer for the Southern Ute Tribe. He held this position for seven years and then, noting his dedication and potential leadership qualities, was elected by his people to the Chairmanship of the Southern Ute Nation in 1966. Thus, he became one of the youngest people to be elected to this position among any of the many Indian Nations across America.

Leonard Burch presently serves on many committees and was appointed by Governor Love of Colorado to the Government's Interstate Council. He is a member of the Board of the American Indian Travel Commission and a commissioner of the Colorado Centennial-Bicentennial Commission.

The Chairman and his wife, with their seven daughters, make their home in Ignacio, Colorado.

LEONARD C. BURCH, Chairman of the Southern Ute Tribal Council.

AT THE TIME OF THE SO-CALLED "discovery" of America, there were living in the mountainous regions of present-day Colorado, northern New Mexico, and eastern Utah a people who came to be known as Utes. They probably came into these areas as a part of a great migration of Indian peoples from western Canada and Alaska during the thirteenth century A.D. Their route was either along the eastern slope of the Rocky Mountains to the Great Plains which they found already inhabited by other Indians, or they filtered into the Colorado Rockies eastward from the Great Basin. The Ute bands, at any rate, had to move into the foothills and mountains where it was much more difficult to hunt animals and gather other foods. Especially in the southern part of the area they were to inhabit there were another people who had lived there since about the beginning of the Christian

1

Era. They are known as the Anasazi (a Navajo word for "the ancient ones") and they had developed from the early Basketmaker through the classic Pueblo stage. Possibly because of the intrusion of the Utes, the Anasazi began to move from mesa tops to sandstone caves for the purposes of defense. In those caves, they built the same type of dwellings that they had been accustomed to build, but because of lack of space, the houses had to be built more compactly and much higher. These houses are known as cliff dwellings which can still be seen in Mesa Verde National Park and other sites in the Four Corners area. Ruins of the early Anasazi culture are to be found all over the present Southern Ute reservation and may presage some economic gains as modern Americans become more and more interested in ancient man in the United States.

If the Utes tried to leave the mountainous area and go other places to get food, they met opposition from other Indian groups already established. To the east and northeast were the Arapahos, Cheyennes, Kiowas, Apaches, Comanches, Sioux, and Pawnees. To the south were the Athabaskan speaking Navajos and Apaches. Only the Jicarilla band of Apaches was generally friendly to the Utes — a friendship that has continued to the present. To the west and northwest were the Shoshones, Snakes, Bannocks, Paiutes, and Goshutes.

The language of the Utes is Shoshonean which is a branch or a dialect of the Uto-Aztecan lan-

2

guage. It is believed that the people who speak Shoshonean separated from other Uto-Aztecan speaking groups about the time of the birth of Christ. Other Indian groups of the United States who speak Shoshonean are the Hopis, Paiutes, Goshutes, Shoshones, Bannocks, and some tribes in California.

Eventually, the Utes became concentrated into a loose confederation of seven bands. The names of the seven bands and the areas in which they lived before the coming of the Europeans are as follows:

1. The *Mouache* band lived in southern Colorado and in New Mexico almost down to Santa Fe.

2. The *Capote* band inhabited the San Luis Valley in Colorado near the headwaters of the Rio Grande and in New Mexico especially around the region where the towns of Chama and Tierra Amarilla are now located.

3. The *Weeminuche* occupied the valley of the San Juan River and its northern tributaries in Colorado and northwestern New Mexico.

4. The *Tabeguache* (also called *Uncompahgre*) lived in the valleys of the Gunnison and Uncompahgre Rivers in Colorado.

5. The Grand River Utes (also called *Parianuc*) lived along that river in Colorado and Utah.

6. The *Yampa* band inhabited the Yampa River Valley and adjacent land.

7. The *Uintah* Utes inhabited the Uintah Basin, especially the western portion.

Of the bands mentioned above, the first two (Mouache and Capote) make up the present day

3

UTE WIGWAM — village scene.

Photograph Courtesy the Smithsonian Institution, Bureau of American Ethnology

Southern Utes with headquarters at Ignacio, Colorado. The Weeminuches are now called the Ute Mountain Utes with headquarters at Towaoc, Colorado. The last four mentioned (Tabeguache, Grand, Yampa, and Uintah) now comprise the Northern Utes on the Uintah-Ouray Reservation with headquarters at the town of Fort Duchesne, Utah. In earlier times, the Grand, Yampa, and Uintah Utes were often referred to as White River Utes.

In aboriginal times, these seven groups of Utes were broken up into small family units for a large portion of each year. It was necessary to do this because food was scarce and it took a large area in the mountains to support a small number of people. Each family unit had to have a great deal of room since food-gathering couldn't be done so well in large groups. From early spring until late in the fall, these family units of Utes would hunt for deer, elk, antelope, and other animals; they would gather seeds of grasses, wild berries and fruits; occasionally they would plant corn, beans, and squash in mountain meadows and harvest them in the autumn. At that time, they did not have horses which would have made the hunting easier nor did they have any tools except those made of stone. Each family unit used to follow a regular circuit during most of the year, going to places where they knew they could gather food for the winter. Older relatives, usually grandparents, were in control of each household unit.

Late in the fall, the family units would begin to

7

move out of the higher mountains into sheltered areas for the winter months. Generally, the family units of a particular band of Utes would live close together during the winter. Each band had its own chief and council. The chiefs or band leaders directed such overall activities as camp movements, defense against enemy raids, war parties, and dances. Family units controlled things pertaining to the individual. The council was composed of the distinguished older men of the various family units and advised the chief on all important matters. The Capotes, Mouache, and Weeminuche would each live through the winter some place in northwestern New Mexico or northeastern Arizona. The Tabeguache or Uncompahgre would select some place between Montrose and Grand Junction. The Northern Utes would live at some place along the White, the Green, or the Colorado Rivers. The winters were great social occasions for the different bands. There would be much visiting and many festivities. This was also the time when marriages would be contracted. For four days in early spring, the band would hold the Bear Dance, the most ancient and typical of all the Ute dances. Then each family unit would prepare to go its separate way until the next winter time. They would follow the migrating deer, antelope, and elk for food until seeds and berries began to ripen in the mountains.

This life style was to be changed for the Utes when the Spaniards colonized New Mexico at the end of the sixteenth century. The reason for this change is

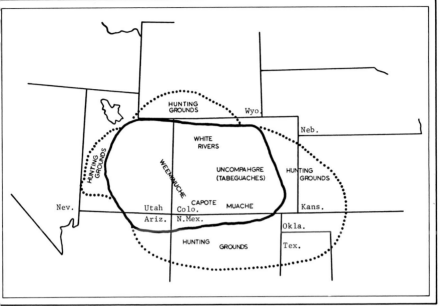

Courtesy of Southern Ute Tribal Council

MAP 1. The Ute Domain.

that although Europeans did not have many of the plants of the Americas, they had livestock and it was livestock, especially the horse, which changed the way of life. Possession of horses allowed the Utes to begin buffalo hunting on the eastern slope of the Rocky Mountains and the buffalo soon became a principal resource, supplying them with an abundance of useful products, *e.g.*, meat for food (one wouldn't have to work so hard hunting deer, elk, and antelope, and gathering seeds and berries), hides for tepee covers, skins for clothing and bedding, stronger moccasins and bags of all types; rawhide for ropes; more sinew thread for sewing and for bowstrings; horns for many purposes, and horn and hoof glue. More particularly, the horse changed the social and political style of the Utes. With the horse, enemies could be evaded more easily, goods could be transported to a central camp where the women and children could be better protected, and the Utes could range further and further afield to get food and products to trade for more horses.

Individually and collectively the Utes were accustomed to trade with neighboring Indian groups. Dried meat and well-tanned animal hides were traded to the Pueblos to the south for agricultural products, cotton blankets, pottery, salt, and turquoise. Indians of the Plains had the products of the buffalo. Hopis had a red ochre paint to trade. Tribes to the west and northwest, who traded with Indians on the Pacific Coast, had sea shells of all types. Apparently, Yavapai, Walapai, and Havasupai

11

traded with the Utes for years before the coming of the Europeans. Actually, products from all over the present-day United States and Mexico reached the Utes by trade along well-established trails, and we have to revise upwards our ideas of the amount of trade carried on in prehistoric times. Northeastern New Mexico and the panhandles of Texas and Oklahoma were familiar to the Utes. Most of the Indian groups were accustomed to raid for captives who could be held for ransom or traded for products. Women and children of other tribes were sought after and adopted into the captors' group partly as a means of getting new blood into the group.

So the Utes no longer needed to spread out thinly in family units. They could live in larger numbers under a more powerful leader. The family unit continued to be the basic unit of society but the leader directed camp movements, hunts, raids, and war parties. In hunting the buffalo the Utes came into frequent contact with the Arapahos, Kiowas, Cheyennes, Sioux, and Comanche who had many more horses than the Utes. The Utes needing these animals became aggressive and warlike. Also, it was much easier to raid for livestock (sheep, goats, cattle) in New Mexico than to hunt deer and other animals, or to buy livestock. So the Utes became raiders, moving out of their mountain fortresses to raid other Indian groups or towns and villages to the south.

THE SPANISH PERIOD

The first European contacts with the Utes came

from the Spanish who probed northward from Mexico City looking for riches and souls to convert to Christianity. It is possible that the early expeditions of Coronado (1540-42), Espejo (1582), and Humaña (1583) met Utes in the northeastern part of New Mexico and elsewhere but numerous Indians were called "Querechos" by those explorers and the word would fit any group of Indians that followed the buffalo and used it as a main source of food. Certainly, the Utes knew of these expeditions and probably began to be acquainted with the horse, metal utensils, and trade trinkets through their traditional trade with the Pueblo and Plains Indians at Taos, Pecos, and Picurís.

Because of the threat posed to the Spanish by Drake's invasion of the Pacific, a desire to protect the rich silver finds in central Mexico and the probability of further riches, it was decided to occupy New Mexico. Accordingly, Juan de Oñate led a group of colonists northward in February, 1598, and five months later established his colony at San Juan de los Caballeros, near the present site of San Juan pueblo. From there, Oñate sent expeditions in every direction to search out the country and the availability of precious minerals. By 1604, Oñate had organized an expedition to search for the Lake of Copala, the legendary ancestral home of some Indian groups in Mexico and Central America and a place of extreme riches. This was near Utah Lake. The expedition under the leadership of Vincente de Zaldívar almost certainly met Utes while going through their lands

13

north and west of Santa Fe following the directions given by Indians of the Jemez pueblo:

> To go straight to the Lake of Copala a guide was not necessary. One must follow the river Chama, and past the tribe of the Navajo Apaches there is a great river which flows to the lake, and with good grass and fields and that in the area between the north and northwest the land was fertile, good and level, and that there are many nations, the province of Quazula, the Qusutas, and further inland another nation settled.

Of course, there was no land of riches but in this and earlier expeditions, the Spanish became acquainted with the Utes and began to describe their life style. In September, 1598, Oñate had sent his nephew, Vincente de Zaldívar, to the buffalo plains to obtain meat for the struggling Spanish colony. Zaldívar met many Indian groups returning from trading with the pueblos of Picurís and Taos. Zaldívar left this description of a camp of fifty tepees made of tanned hides. In all probability, it was a Ute encampment.

> They were . . . very bright red and white in color and bell shaped, with flags and openings, and built as skillfully as those of Italy and so large that in the most ordinary ones four different mattresses and beds were easily accommodated. The tanning is so fine that although it should rain bucketfulls it will not pass through nor stiffen the hide, but rather upon drying it remains as soft and pliable as before.

Zaldívar's description of the men and the women of the Utes indicated that:

> Most of the men were said to go naked, probably with breechcloths, but the women wore sort of trousers of buckskin and 'shoes and leggins, after their own fashion.' They would hold a piece of meat, almost raw, in one hand,

14

and a piece of suet in the other. The suet was used as bread. They would take a bite of the meat and then one of the bread. On this diet they were said to grow very strong and courageous. As weapons they had a spear with a long thick point, and arrows tipped with flint which were 'better than spears to kill cattle.' They were said to be very skillful with the bow and arrow and were able to kill a buffalo with the first shot. These Indians would hide themselves in blinds of brush near watering places and ambush the buffalo as they came to drink.

Again, Zaldivar described the use of dogs as beasts of burden by the Utes:

> It is a sight worth seeing and very laughable to see them travelling, the ends of the poles dragging on the ground, nearly all of them snarling in their encounters, to load them the Indian women seize their heads between their knees and thus load them or adjust the load, which is seldom required, because they travel along at a steady gait as if they had been trained by means of a rein.

The Utes, or Yutas as they came to be called by the Spanish, are mentioned often enough in early Spanish documents to indicate that they were quite well known to the Spanish settlements in New Mexico. Father Zarate Salmeron mentioned them specifically for the first time in 1626. He wrote about the province of Quazula, where the Yutas lived, and the Colorado River, which ran through their territory and was said to be populated thickly all the way to its source. Other reports indicate that Oñate encountered Yutas on his 1604-05 expedition to the Gulf of California but the Indian groups known today as Ute, Southern Paiute, Chemehuevi, Kaibabits, Shivwits and others who spoke Uto-Aztecan

15

languages were all called Yutas by the Spaniards at that time.

At any rate, the Spanish came to know the Utes and Ute territory. They saw them trading with Pueblo Indians under the charge of Spanish Franciscan missionaries at Pecos, Taos, Picurís, and other places. The Utes came to know the use of the horse and began to raid other Indian groups for captives to be exchanged for horses and other products. Probably, these practices caused the earliest known conflict between the Utes and the Spaniards. Luís de Rosas, governor of New Mexico from 1637 to 1641, captured about eighty "Utacas" (probably Mouaches) of the upper Rio Grande and forced them to labor in a work shop established by him in Santa Fe.

Intermittent contacts followed; the Spaniards obtaining more captives and the Utes gaining more horses and other products. With increased mobility, the Utes increased their range of activities and began to travel in larger bands. By 1670, the Spanish found it convenient to arrange a peace treaty with the Utes who were described as equals to Apaches and a people who did not turn their back on combat. This treaty was apparently still in effect when the Pueblo Indians rose in revolt in 1680 and drove the Spanish out of New Mexico to the present-day area of El Paso. During the twelve years that the Spanish were out of New Mexico the Capote Utes extended their southern border to the San Juan River and the Mouache Utes began to attack Taos and the Tewa villages between Española and Santa Fe and travel in

16

TE WINTER HOME in Navajo Springs, Colorado. The poles at the right were used in the ummertime for a tepee which was covered with skins during chilly weather and with brush uring hot weather. The Utes were described in 1598 as living in thatch covered huts. After 1ey acquired the horse, they became tepee dwellers. As they became more sedentary and onfined to reservations, they built winter homes similar to the one pictured above. Now ery modern housing is seen throughout the reservation.

large bands to the plains to obtain Pawnee captives. Without Spanish protection, the Pueblos were no match for the fast moving, raiding Utes.

By the time the Spanish reoccupied New Mexico in 1692, the Utes were highly respected and even feared by the Pueblos and all neighboring tribes. In 1694, Mouache Utes attacked Spanish troops under Governor Diego de Vargas on the San Antonio River near the present Colorado-New Mexico border. The skirmish was quick and the Utes apologized explaining that Pueblo Indians had been coming into Ute country dressed in Spanish clothes and Vargas' company of soldiers were thought to be another such group. Apparently, Governor de Vargas accepted this explanation for he invited the Utes to come to Santa Fe to trade as they had done before the Pueblo Revolt of 1680.

In the early 1700's, the village of Española (La Cañada) became the main center for trading Spanish products with the Utes. Of course, they were regular participants at the yearly Taos fair where many different Indian groups met to exchange necessary products. To deny an Indian tribe the right to engage in trading activities at the yearly fair usually meant war.

Indians who lived close to the Pueblo Indians of New Mexico, including the Utes, constantly disrupted Spanish control of and arrangements with those Pueblos. Spanish officials always had to guard against any possible alliance between the Pueblos and the Utes or other frontier Indians for the safety of the

19

Spanish population of New Mexico. The Spanish were generally unsuccessful, because the Utes and other tribes continued to raid the Pueblos.

The increased mobility, especially of the Mouache Utes, had led to excursions to the north and east and had brought the Utes into frequent contact with the Comanches. Around 1700, the Utes and their kinsmen, the Comanches, began to raid the Pueblos for horses, agricultural products, and captives to be held for ransom. The full force of Ute and Comanche attacks were felt from 1696 to 1727 especially in the north central and northeastern portions of New Mexico. In 1719, the peace between the Utes and the Spanish was broken. Governor Antonio Valverde Cossio of New Mexico carried on an extensive campaign against them after a Council of War and opinions gathered from Spanish leaders in Santa Fe. That punitive expedition against the Utes and Comanches was largely unsuccessful and the Spanish turned to developing peace with the Jicarilla Apaches who would act as a buffer state.

From about 1650 the Apaches had been gradually encroaching on Ute lands and, by the time of the return of the Spanish, had settled in the Sierra Blancas north of Taos and in northeast New Mexico. Because the Spanish offered some protection, the Utes were willing to form an alliance with them. When this alliance broke down, the Utes and the Comanches began raiding the Jicarillas, burning rancherías and capturing women and children to sell for ransom.

20

The Ute alliance with the Comanches lasted intemittently from 1700 to 1746 to help apply pressure against the encroaching Apache. So from about 1700 to 1750, relations among the Utes, Comanches, Apaches and Spanish were confused, shifting from warfare to alliance and back again. By the end of the Ute-Comanche alliance, and one of the reasons for its ending, the Apaches had been driven out of northeastern New Mexico and into an area south and west of the Ute lands.

By 1748, the Comanches had become strong enough to turn on their Ute allies and cause problems for the Spanish as well. To end this problem the governor of New Mexico, Joachín de Coadallos y Rabal, marched on both the Utes and Comanches and defeated them in a battle above Abiquiu, New Mexico. After this a series of battles between the Utes and the Spanish lasted for two years before the Utes came to Taos to sue for peace with the Spanish. The Utes were finding it too difficult to fight both the Spanish and the Comanches. They also needed the trade in horses that the Spanish could provide. In 1750, peace between the Utes and the Spanish was obtained.

Trading, trapping and exploration brought renewed interest in the land north of Taos. With the peace of 1750 the Spanish were able to re-establish Abiquiu as a point of departure to the north. From Abiquiu the Spanish were then able to send trading parties into the Ute country to trade for the soft deerskins that the Utes were able to provide. The

Spanish also became interested in trapping the numerous rivers of the Ute nation for fur bearing animals, a product that was in great demand in Europe. Finally, the Spanish were still interested in the land of Copala and its potential wealth and locating an overland route through that area to the West Coast.

Almost immediately after Abiquiu had been re-established, trading parties were sent to trade with the Utes. In 1765, Juan María de Rivera was sent across the San Juan River and along the Uncompahgre Plateau to the Gunnison River to trade and trap for furs. During the next ten years Rivera led three other expeditions into the Ute lands. Others who explored the region to the north of New Mexico were Nicolas de la Fora in 1766-67, and Pedro Mora with Gregorio Sandoval and Andrés Muñiz in 1775.

In addition to their interest in the Utes, the Spanish were looking for a land route to the Pacific Ocean where the new capital of California had been established at Monterey in 1770. A plan for locating the route was first conceived by Fray Silvestre Vélez de Escalante when he was visiting the Hopis in 1775, and Escalante was greatly encouraged to hear from the Franciscan Padre Garcés who had been operating in Arizona and California:

> It is possible to proceed through the Yutas (Utes) and seek the Rio de San Felipe, and down the banks of this will be found my road (to California). I doubt not that there may open another, better, and shorter than that which I traced.

Escalante and Fray Atanasio Domínguez, the

expedition leader, chose the route through the Ute lands rather than risk encounters with the unfriendly Navajos. The route was well known to the Spanish, and guides were available who knew the Utes and their language and had seen parts of their country.

Escalante's trip into the interior of the Ute domain was the first one that extended into the mythical land of Copala. He found the area thought to be Copala poor and unproductive for the desires of the Spanish. Neither gold nor silver were located, and they did not find the route to Monterey. They did, however, explore much of the Ute domain.

The route the expedition took led them up the valley of the Chama River past Abiquiu to the site of Tierra Amarilla, thence to the place where Pagosa Springs now stands. (Pagosa in Ute means hot water.) After crossing the Dolores River below the San Juan Mountains the party traveled to the Uncompahgre Plateau and down the Uncompahgre River to its confluence with the Gunnison. From this point their route took the expedition along the western slope of the Rockies to the White River in northern Colorado. At that point the group turned west across Utah just south of the Uinta mountains to Utah Lake. From there they turned south through the southern Paiute lands, to Zuñi and then on to Santa Fé. Escalante was convinced this route offered a shorter, better method for reaching Monterey.

Although Escalante failed to find the riches of the land of Copala, his expedition was important for the exploration of country unknown to the Spanish and for the locating of the Indian groups that lived in the present-day states of Colorado and Utah. This penetration into Ute land marked the beginning of a new era for the Utes. No longer was their land considered an unknown area. Now people would journey from Santa Fe far into the interior of the Ute domain to trade.

The Spanish felt a stronger tie to the Utes after Escalante's expedition and continued to cultivate their friendship and alliance. In 1779, 200 Mouache Utes and Jicarilla Apaches joined Governor Juan Bautista de Anza in a campaign against the Comanche who had been raiding the settlements of New Mexico. A peace between the groups was not established until 1786 when the Utes, the Comanches and the Spanish met at Pecos. This alliance and past experiences caused the Spanish to look to the Utes for assistance when either the Comanches or the Navajos raided the Spanish settlements. In support of these alliances a second peace treaty between the Utes and the Spanish was signed in 1789.

The Navajos had caused trouble for both the Spanish and the Utes for many years. Ute-Navajo relations varied according to the need of both groups for protection from outside raiding groups. If either tribe was threatened by a group of Plains Indians an alliance was struck. When this outside threat was not great, the two groups would raid one another and compete for the land that was common to both tribes. During these periods the Navajos often formed an alliance with the Apaches or with a Pueblo tribe to

24

raid the Utes, and the Utes banded together with Plains groups such as the Comanche. At other times the Spanish would form an alliance with the Utes against the Navajo to defend the Pueblo Indians of New Mexico. The treaty of 1789 was made by the Spanish with the Utes to insure this alliance against the Navajos. At the same time, the Navajos and the Utes were enjoying a period of good relations. It was not until 1804 that history records a campaign of an alliance of Mouache Utes, Jicarilla Apaches and Spanish against the Navajos. As in the past the Utes remained friendly to the Spaniards and acted as a check against raids by the Navajo, Comanches, and Apaches.

Two years after the 1804 alliance, the first known citizen of the newly created country of the United States of America arrived in the San Luis Valley, in the heart of Ute country, and was guided to Santa Fé by two Mouache Utes. Zebulon Montgomery Pike's appearance marked the beginning of a new era for the Ute Indians. Soon the Spanish with their trading expeditions sent into the Ute domain would be replaced, first by Mexican traders and then by American traders and trappers and later American settlers coming to occupy the land.

The transition from Spanish to Mexican control of the Ute lands went almost unnoticed by the Ute Indians. The pattern of trading established by the Spanish and the amount of contact between the two groups continued as before. The Spanish had been very careful to create peaceful relations with the

A VIEW OF SOUTHERN UTE COSTUME in the last century. Note the large infant cradleboard at the left, both men and women wearing concho belts, moccasins, fringed buckskins, and

e continued use of bone breastplates.

powerful Ute nation and the Mexicans continued the practice.

THE MEXICAN PERIOD: 1821-48

To encourage peace, the Mexican government distributed gifts to the Utes throughout the 1820s, because at no time in the Mexican period did the government in New Mexico have enough troops to control the frontier tribes. This policy apparently paid off for in 1829 the "Old Spanish Trail" was inaugurated between Santa Fé and San Gabriel, California. Mule trains would depart from Abiquiu, move up the Chama River, cross over to the San Juan and then continue on westward in Utah and Arizona. A northern branch of the trail was later developed which passed through Cochetopa Pass. There were many variations to the "Old Spanish Trail"; sometimes the route went as far north in Utah as Utah Lake but a large part always went through Ute territory, and the Utes became accustomed to trade their products including captives captured from other Indian groups.

As with other Indian groups in the United States familiarity of non-Indians with the Ute Territory resulted in a desire to own parts of that territory. Mexicans travelling the "Old Spanish Trail" found beautiful valleys in the Ute domain which would be almost perfect for ranching and other purposes. The Mexican government began to make grants of land to Mexican citizens which resulted in the lessening of the land base of the Utes and the beginning of a rising

29

TRANSPORTATION OF THE UTES progressed from human burden bearing to pack dogs to horses for riding and packing to wagons and buggies and finally to the modern pickup and

passenger automobiles used today.

tide of anger by those Indians. The Tierra Amarilla grant was allotted in July, 1832, covering the region from the Rio Nutrias, a tributary of the Chama, northward to the Navajo River, a tributary of the upper San Juan. This grant took a considerable area considered by the Capote Utes to be theirs. The valley of the Conejos River, a tributary to the upper Rio Grande, was another place desired by the Mexicans who unsuccessfully attempted to settle there in 1833 and again ten years later the Mouache Utes prevented another attempted settlement there, a process they had to repeat in 1851, shortly after the United States takeover. Other grants by the Mexican government in northern New Mexico and southern Colorado speeded up the process of the erosion of the Ute land base, and was to result in trouble later on.

The United States agreed to respect all valid land grants by terms of the treaty of Guadalupe-Hidalgo (1848) which ended the war with Mexico. They had been granted by the Spanish and Mexican governments to petitioners who agreed to develop the land and to protect the frontier. Many of the land grants adversely affected different bands of Utes. For example, the very large and famous Maxwell Land Grant of over one and one-half million acres in the northeastern portion of New Mexico and southeastern Colorado included some former Ute holdings; the San Joaquin del Cañon del Rio de Chama Grant had given land to settlers near Abiquiu, as did the Cañon de San Miguel (Pedernales) Grant; in the area of present day Colorado, the Las Animas Grant embraced the land south of the Arkansas River to the Sangre de Cristos between the Huerfano and Purgatory Rivers (Ceran St. Vrain and Cornelio Vigil); the Sangre de Cristo Grant covered a large area in the lower San Luis Valley; the Conejos Grant took away from the Utes the western portion of the San Luis Valley; and the Tierra Amarilla Grant extended from that town into southern Colorado. Although never heavily populated by Europeans, these grants by the Spanish and Mexican governments led to continuous friction.

Another result of the independence of Mexico from Spain for the Utes was exposure to a new group of aggressive traders and trappers from the United States who no longer had to evade the restrictions and inflexibility of Spanish commercial law and who found it much easier to deal with Mexican authorities in Santa Fé than with the former Spanish officials. The Santa Fé Trail was opened in 1821 between Independence, Missouri and Santa Fé and the Utes could see that cheaper and better goods could be procured as a result of the increased trade. In 1822, the Ute chief Lechat went to Santa Fé and expressed a desire to trade directly with the Anglo-Americans and he pointed out the superiority of some Ute goods over those of the local Mexicans but nothing immediate seems to have come of his proposal.

The principal contact of the Anglo-Americans with the Utes, however, was to come from the "Mountain Men" and fur trappers who had recognized that the Ute domain contained numerous mountain streams abounding in beaver. The process of trapping began even under the domination by Spain. In 1811, Ezekiel Williams was trapping for beaver pelts in southwestern Colorado and the following year Robert McKnight was in the same region. In 1816 and 1817, Auguste Pierre Chouteau and Julius DeMunn had moved into southwestern Colorado for the same purpose. The numbers of trappers in Ute territory increased tremendously in the Mexican period. In 1821, Col. Hugh Glenn and Jacob Fowler led a trapping expedition into the San Luis Valley and possibly even into present Archuleta and Mineral counties of Colorado. In 1824, William Becknell, "The Father of the Santa Fe Trade," led a party of trappers to the Green River and William Huddart headed an expedition of fourteen men from Taos to the same area. Probably both expeditions traveled along the western slope of the Colorado Rockies through Ute country. At about the same time, Kit Carson and Jason Lee left New Mexico and went to the Uinta River in Utah, where they met Antoine Robidoux. In 1826, James Ohio Pattie passed through the present site of Grand Junction in Mesa County, Colorado, after departing from Santa Fé, going south to the Gila River and following that river to the Colorado River and then ascending that river into Ute territory.

In the 1830s, beaver pelts became even more valuable and many more fur trappers and traders entered Colorado and Utah. In 1832, Antoine

Robidoux, a fur trader from St. Louis, Missouri, established Fort Uncompahgre, a fort and fur trading post just below the junction of the Gunnison and Uncompahgre Rivers near the present site of Delta, Colorado; and he later established a similar outfitting and trading post on the Uinta River in Utah. Philip Thompson and William Craig founded Fort Davy Crockett on the Green River in 1837. None of these trading posts in Ute country prospered. The Utes burned Fort Uncompahgre and about 1840 Fort Davy Crockett was abandoned right after Kit Carson and James Baker had headquartered there through the fall and winter of 1839-40. In 1842, Rufus Sage left Taos, passed through southwestern Colorado to the post on the Uinta, probably passing along the old Ute trail through Archuleta and La Plata counties.

Thus the whole country of the Utes became known to Anglo-Americans and the Utes became acquainted with their products. The fur trappers and traders from the United States were generally on very friendly terms with the Ute people. The Indians were willing to trade buffalo robes and beaver pelts for flour, cloth, tobacco, trinkets, and even illegal whiskey. Buffalo robes and beaver pelts were readily sold in the eastern part of the United States and in Europe. Most of the trappers and traders had lived for long periods of time with Indian groups and they were diplomats who could barter successfully, and generally fairly, with the Utes. The Utes welcomed them into their territory because they knew that they were not permanent settlers. The take-over by the

36

United States of all Ute lands occurred at the same time as a drastic reduction in the value of furs because the French silk had replaced the felt hat formerly worn by gentlemen, and ladies began to prefer seal-skin coats to fur coats that the Rocky Mountains could supply. Many of the trappers and traders, therefore, soon took employment as scouts for the United States Army and they were to prove invaluable in dealing with the Indians of the West.

This is true partly because one valuable contribution of the Utes was the sharing of their knowledge regarding the topography of the mountainous region they inhabited. After years as a food-gathering people, the Utes had thoroughly learned the paths of least resistance to travel — the lowest passes in the many chains of mountains and the ridges which were easiest to cross. The friction of their feet over centuries had cut deep trails along the most important routes of travel. Where trails intersected or became difficult to follow in the rocky terrain, the Utes were accustomed to build stone monuments in prominent places eight to ten feet high with a stone on top pointing out the right direction. Pioneers, road builders, and railroad builders were to use these to a great advantage. A look at any map showing the transportation routes in Ute country will indicate to the casual observer the trails formerly used extensively by the Utes in their travels.

In the late Mexican period, relations between the settlers in New Mexico and the Utes were often unsettled and unfriendly. The Utes, seeing their land holdings diminishing because of increased ranching and farming, periodically raided the settlements for livestock and other articles. A rising level of anger impelled the Utes to more and more depredations. In 1846, the United States entered into a war against Mexico, the result of which was going to be the incorporation of all Ute territory into the United States. Thus the United States had to begin dealing with the Utes as the Spanish and Mexican governments had to do before. Only two years before, Utes had created a sensation in Santa Fé by threatening the governor of New Mexico in the Palace of the Governors, an event well known to the Anglo-Americans. From then until the American takeover in 1846, the Mexican government at Santa Fé generally was at war with the Utes, who, mounted on good horses and with firearms, raided the Taos Valley and the frontier around Abiquiu.

THE U.S. DOMINANCE

Groundwork for the takeover of the southwestern portion of the United States, which included a large area of the Ute domain, had been laid by Santa Fé traders and the Mountain Men and fur trappers during the late Spanish period and throughout the entire Mexican period. Observers could see that the control of the Mexican government was exceedingly tenuous and that the whole area could be taken by a very few aggressive men. The idea of "Manifest Destiny" was rampant throughout the United States and this idea was largely responsible for the war between the United States and Mexico, 1846-48.

As soon as the war was begun, United States forces moved to occupy the present-day states of New Mexico, Arizona, and California. Of concern to the military leaders was the possibility that Utes, different bands of whom could operate as an efficient light cavalry, might cut the lines of communication. This possibility was not just conjecture because by 1827 the Mouache Utes and their allies, the Jicarilla Apaches, had been openly hostile to Santa Fé traders in northeastern New Mexico along the last part of the trail into Santa Fé. Sporadic raids by these Indians had made the traders very cautious and suspicious of the Utes.

Within a month after the conquest of New Mexico and as General S. W. Kearny moved to take California, William Gilpin was sent from Santa Fé to confer with Ute leaders. Gilpin carried out his assignment by travelling through northern New Mexico and southern Colorado, especially in the San Luis Valley, contacting different bands of Utes. He succeeded in inducing sixty Ute headsmen to accompany him to Santa Fé to confer with United States military authorities there. After a conference in Santa Fe with Col. Alexander W. Doniphan, the Ute leaders agreed to remain peaceful.

On December 30, 1849, the first treaty between the Utes and the United States was signed at Abiquiu, the frontier town on the Chama River north of the town of Española. This treaty was arranged largely by the great Indian agent, James S. Calhoun.

The Utes recognized the sovereignty of the United States and agreed not to depart from their accustomed territory without permission. The Utes also agreed to perpetual peace and friendship with the United States, to abide by United States law, and to permit citizens of the United States government to establish military posts and agencies in their country. Quiziachigiate signed as principal chief and twenty-seven other Utes signed as subordinate chiefs.

After the twenty-eight Ute leaders expressed an "utter aversion to labor," Agent Calhoun promised that the United States would help take care of the Utes to the amount of $5,000 per year. No boundaries of the Ute territory were defined in this treaty.

The following year (1850) the United States government opened an agency for the Utes at Taos, New Mexico. John Greiner was the first agent (1851-53), but the United States failed to provide the necessary money and the agency had to close. It was reopened in December, 1853, largely to serve the Capote band of Utes, and Kit Carson, the famous trapper, mountain man and trader, who was a friend to the Utes, was named agent. He served in that capacity until 1859. The Mouache band of Utes was also served at the Taos agency during the time, but members of the Weeminuche band came there infrequently. The Tabeguache band of Utes heard of rations being allotted to their relatives and went to Taos in 1856. Kit Carson recommended that an agency for the Tabeguache be set up closer to their country but his request was not acted on by the

United States for several years. Kit Carson (1809-1868) was the best known of the fur trappers and traders who had entered Ute territory. While a young man, he had trapped for eight years in South Park and had become familiar with practically every Ute trail and every pass in the mountains. He was modest and amiable and the Indians generally considered him a worthwhile friend, especially because he had married Singing Grass, an Arapaho, while very young, and at Taos, in 1843, had married Josefa Jaramillo.

Between 1851 and 1853, towns were founded in the San Luis Valley (San Luis, San Pedro, and San Acacia) by former Mexican citizens. As usual with the influx of settlers, livestock was introduced and the supply of game animals began to diminish or to move to more inaccessible places in the mountains. Also it was much easier for the Utes to raid for livestock than to hunt game in those higher altitudes. Bad blood increased between the Utes and the settlers, and the usual patterns of raid, followed by punitive expeditions, were established in southern Colorado.

To safeguard the settlers and to keep the Utes from raiding, the United States government established Fort Massachusetts on Ute Creek near the base of Mt. Blanca. (Six years later that military post was moved six miles south and renamed Fort Garland.)

The Utes did not like either the military post in the midst of their territory or the presence of the settlers, whose farming and ranching began to drive out the game upon which the Utes depended for part of their food supply. Their resentment flared in the Ute War of 1854-55. On Christmas Day of 1854, the Utes attacked Fort Pueblo on the Arkansas River and killed all the inhabitants. Then they began attacking the settlements in the San Luis Valley. Several settlers were killed and their livestock driven away. Fort Massachusetts was severely threatened. General Garland at Santa Fé was notified and he quickly organized six companies of mounted volunteers from New Mexico plus some units of regular troops and sent them to Fort Massachusetts to put down the Ute revolt. Col. Thomas T. Fauntleroy was placed in command and Kit Carson accompanied the expedition as head scout.

The leader of the Utes was Chief Tierra Blanca, who was easily recognized because of the red shirt which he wore. The United States troops made their first contact with the Utes near the present town of Salida, in the Saguache Valley, in the middle of March, 1855. The Utes, recognizing the superior fire power of the United States troops, retreated in a running fight toward Cochetopa Pass and most of that band escaped. Another band of Utes was, however, surprised near Salida. About forty of them were killed and some livestock recovered on April 19, 1855. Throughout the remainder of April and for the next two months, running battles and skirmishes occurred, but the Utes recognized that they could not continue to fight the forces of the United States and asked for peace. A meeting was held at Abiquiu,

42

GROUP OF SOUTHERN UTE WOMEN in front of a tepee, which includes Chipeta, the wife
Chief Ouray.

mainly with the Capote Utes, and a treaty of peace was arranged in the fall of 1855.

Also in 1855, a treaty was negotiated with the Mouaches at Abiquiu. Had that treaty been ratified by the United States Senate, the Mouaches would have been placed on a reservation of 1000 square miles in the extreme northern part of the Territory of New Mexico with the Rio Grande as the eastern boundary and the mountains between the drainages of the Rio Grande and the San Juan River as the western boundary.

After the United States acquired California there was a general interest in building a transcontinental railroad. The issue became entangled in the controversy between the North and the South but several surveys for the best route were authorized by the Congress. Of course, one big obstacle to the building of the railroad was the mass of mountains in the west. Two such surveys explored the mountainous area of the Utes.

In 1848, John C. Fremont attempted to cross the San Juan Mountains to find a suitable route for a transcontinental railroad. Many of his party met disaster near La Garita before being rescued by former mountain men from Taos. In 1853, Captain John W. Gunnison was ordered by Secretary of War Jefferson Davis to survey the most practicable route for a transcontinental railroad. The huge party which accompanied Captain Gunnison explored and mapped Ute territory to a greater extent than ever before. Captain Gunnison was killed by the Utes in western

Utah, but Lt. E. G. Beckwith continued in command and wrote an account of the expedition. Both Captain Gunnison and Lt. Beckwith were of the opinion that the Ute lands west of San Luis Valley were of no value for settlement by Anglo-Americans.

Less than five years after that statement was made, gold was discovered near the present site of Denver and the "Rush to the Rockies" was in progress.

Thousands of Anglo-Americans from the Missouri and the Mississippi Valleys with "Pike's Peak or Bust" painted on the canvas of their wagons poured into the area of Colorado. Many returned with "Busted by God" on their wagons, but enough remained to organize the Territory of Colorado in 1861. The governor of the territory, William Gilpin, appointed by the President, was named to be Superintendent of Indian Affairs within the territory. Thus, by 1861, the Utes came under the local control of the governors of the territories of Colorado, Utah, and New Mexico.

In 1861, an agency was opened at Conejos, Colorado, under Agent Lafayette Head for the Tabeguache Utes, but he was hampered by lack of funds. The agency at Taos continued to operate for the Capotes, Mouaches, and Weeminuches. As throughout the history of the United States, the migration of miners and settlers into a new region caused trouble between them and the Indians accustomed to hunt and gather food. The white settlers could not understand why the Indians should need so

46

much land, and the Indians regarded the newcomers as interlopers and trespassers. Because of the friction which was developing in Colorado, a conference was held at the agency in Conejos on October 1, 1863. The representatives of all the Ute bands were to have been at the conference, but the Northern Utes sent insufficient representation.

The United States was represented at the conference by Simeon Whiteley, agent for the Northern Utes from Hot Sulphur Springs; Lafayette Head, agent for the Tabeguaches at Conejos; Michael Steck, superintendent of the Southern Ute agency at Taos; John Evans, governor of the Territory of Colorado, and John Nicolay, secretary to President Abraham Lincoln, from Washington, D.C. Mr. Nicolay served as secretary of this commission, whose aim was to move the Utes out of the path of the miners and settlers. Inasmuch as the Northern Utes were not well represented, the commission dealt only with the Tabeguache Utes and the Mouache band of Southern Utes. The Tabeguache refused to be moved to a new location but did agree to a treaty which defined the boundaries of a reservation for them and the Mouaches. Ten Tabeguache leaders, including Ouray, signed this treaty by which they gave up claim to much land already occupied by white settlers in return for promises of livestock and goods for the next ten years.

The United States government failed to provide the Tabeguache with any of the goods promised in the treaty and the Tabeguache continued to live in their accustomed places. In 1864, heavy snows prevented them from hunting buffalo in the plains and foothills for their winter supply of meat, and the Tabeguaches were reduced to begging around Colorado City. This caused friction with the white people, and more developed in the San Luis Valley between the Utes and the settlers there. The United States government determined to settle the Ute question and remove them, especially from the San Luis Valley.

To accomplish this, a treaty was negotiated on March 2, 1868, at Washington, D.C. The United States was represented by Governor A. C. Hunt for the Territory of Colorado, N. G. Taylor, and Kit Carson. The seven bands of Utes who sent representatives were the Tabeguache, Mouache, Capote, Weemiuche, Yampa, Grand River and Uintah.

By this treaty, a single reservation was provided for all the Ute bands and the area comprised roughly the western one-third of Colorado. An agency for the three bands of Northern Utes was to be established on the White River near the present town of Meeker, Colorado. Another agency was to be established on the Los Pinos River for the Tabeguaches, Mouaches, Capotes, and Weeminuches. Education, clothing, and rations were to be provided by the United States until the Utes should be capable of supporting themselves. The Utes were assured that this reservation would forever be theirs and they would be protected from white trespassers. This treaty was signed by the ten Ute leaders and it was

48

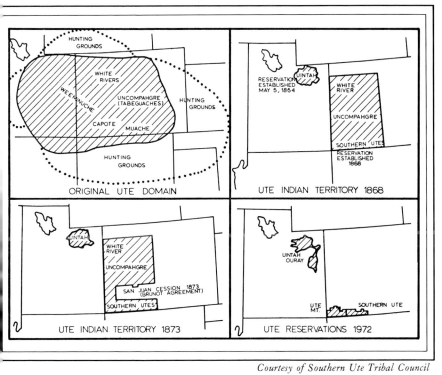

ORIGINAL UTE DOMAIN

HUNTING GROUNDS
WHITE RIVERS
WE-E-MINUCHE
UNCOMPAHGRE (TABEGUACHES)
HUNTING GROUNDS
CAPOTE MUACHE
HUNTING GROUNDS

UTE INDIAN TERRITORY 1868

RESERVATION ESTABLISHED MAY 5, 1864
UINTAH
WHITE RIVER
UNCOMPAHGRE
SOUTHERN UTES
RESERVATION ESTABLISHED 1868

UTE INDIAN TERRITORY 1873

UINTAH
WHITE RIVER
UNCOMPAHGRE
SAN JUAN CESSION 1873 (BRUNOT AGREEMENT)
SOUTHERN UTES

UTE RESERVATIONS 1972

UINTAH OURAY
UTE MT.
SOUTHERN UTE

Courtesy of Southern Ute Tribal Council

MAP 2. Ute Domain Reservations.

at this time that Ouray was selected by the United States to be spokesman for the Utes instead of Colorow or another headsman whom the Northern Utes preferred.

It appeared that the Treaty of 1868 would settle the "Ute problem," but such was not the case. The Tabeguache band started to go to the Los Pinos River, but they refused to go further when they arrived at a branch of Cochetopa Creek about sixty miles to the north and about fifty-five miles west of Saguache, Colorado. This spot was not even on the specified reservation but the United States set up the Los Pinos agency there, naming the tributary of Cochetopa Creek "Los Pinos" to comply with the letter of the treaty, which had meant the Rio de Los Pinos, the tributary of Las Animas River in present-day La Plata County, named by the Spaniards in the eighteenth century. Also, almost immediately after the treaty was negotiated, it was discovered that the San Juan Mountains of southwestern Colorado held huge treasures of rich minerals.

Actually, a third agency was maintained at Denver from 1871 to 1876 for the Utes of that area. During those years, the Utes still hunted buffalo there for the winter supply of meat and sold hides and other products to merchants. By the time that Colorado became a state of the Union in 1876, the huge herds of buffalo had been largely eliminated from the plains and the Utes around Denver had no products to sell and no more money to buy goods from the

51

merchants. Soon their presence in the capital city became a source of friction and trouble.

By the Act of April 10, 1869, Congress paved the way for President Grant to end all troubles with Indians by settling the remaining Indians on reservations deemed large enough to support them if they engaged in agriculture.

THE CREATION OF THE RESERVATION

In 1868, the geographic locations of the three bands of the Southern Utes had changed little from the time when the first Spaniard had entered their domain. During the Mexican period the bands were moved closer together, and their use of the plains as hunting grounds was restricted. These changes seem, however, due more to pressure on the Utes from the Comanches and Apaches than from either the Spanish, Mexicans, or the first Americans who entered the region.

The 700 Weeminuches lived in an area that stretched from Tierra Amarilla northward to the Las Animas River and on to the Colorado River. Their chiefs were Peersichopa and Cabegon. The headmen included Sewormicha, Piwood, Ignacio, Chiwaten, and Tobats. The bands of Cabegon and Sewormicha cultivated the land along the La Plata River, one of the few groups of Utes to grow some of their own food rather than trade for it. For the most part they were self-supporting with only a few of the band visiting the agency at Tierra Amarilla. Supplies received from the government included powder, lead, salt, and blankets. Their hunting grounds were located west of the San Juan headwaters and their lodges on the Las Animas, the La Plata, and the Mancos rivers. They traded bear, deer, beaver, and a few otter skins for horses, sugar, and coffee. In turn, the horses were traded to the Mouache Utes located at Cimarron in exchange for buffalo robes and the skins to the Navajos for blankets. Of the three major bands of the Southern Utes, the Weeminuche remained the most isolated from Anglo contact.

The 484 Mouache occupied the San Luis Valley as well as the east side of the Sangre de Cristo Mountains north of Taos. They were given supplies from the Cimarron agency and occasionally the Abiquiu agency. In 1869, an agency on the Conejos River was established for these people. The new location was considered a more practical distribution point for the goods given to the band.

The 500 Capotes lived in an area ranging north from Abiquiu to the Navajo River with Tierra Amarilla being the central location for most of the band. The agency at Abiquiu was the distribution point for government goods for the band although some rations were received at Tierra Amarilla. Of the three bands the Capotes seemed to rely most on government for survival. The one exception was the group under the leadership of Sapota. His people, about sixty-five in number, stayed near the San Juan River most of the time and rarely ventured south to either Abiquiu or Tierra Amarilla. His hunting skill was so great that he was able to provide game for nearly all of the needs of his people. Other leaders of the Capotes at this time included Timpioche and Chorez.

In 1863, a reservation had been defined for the Utes, although little attempt was made to restrict the Utes to this land. After 1868, the three Ute bands were forced to occupy much smaller territories. The reduction of this reservation in 1868 came not from pressure of other Indian tribes but rather from the pressure of the Anglos. One of the Anglo groups pressuring the Utes onto smaller territories was the miners. Gold had been discovered near Denver, Colorado, in 1859. Soon prospectors were spanning out from the area towards the mountains to the south and the west looking for more of the precious mineral. By 1860, a group of miners had entered the western slope of Colorado and had located gold in the San Juan mountains of southwest Colorado in the heart of Ute land. After the Ute treaty of 1868 miners came in increasing numbers to find the rich minerals of this region. In direct violation of the previous Ute treaties miners trespassed on the reservation.

The Federal Government, unable to stop the invasion of Anglos, responded to the crisis by calling the Ute leaders together. The Government tried to negotiate with the Indians for the land occupied by the miners. Congress had passed a law in 1871 stating that the Government would no longer sign treaties with the Indians but rather would now sign agreements. The change in terminology meant little to the Indians for the meaning was the same; the Government wanted the Utes' land. In 1873, the Utes signed the Brunot agreement, in which they gave up their claim to the San Juan mountains. The agreement, also known as the San Juan Cession, was signed into law by President Ulysses S. Grant in 1874.

The land taken by the government was rectangular in shape and included the middle section of the 1868 reservation. Now only a narrow strip of land along the western boundary of the state of Colorado connected the northern part of the 1868 reservation with the southern part. The southern part of the reservation was now a section of land 110 miles long, running from the Utah boundary east along the New Mexico-Colorado border, and fifteen miles wide, beginning with the New Mexico boundary and running due north.

For some time the Anglos of northern New Mexico had wanted to move those Southern Utes located at Cimarron and Abiquiu onto the southern portion of the Ute reservation. The Brunot agreement of 1874 had stated that all of the Mouache and Capote Utes not located on the reservation in Colorado were to be moved there and an agency created for them. Originally, the agency was to be located on the southern portion of the reservation so the Southern Utes could reach it without travelling long distances. One agency had been located north of the San Juan

Cession but had been so far from the Southern Utes that they had refused to travel there for their rations. Instead they remained in New Mexico.

In 1875, the agent at Cimarron, Alexander G. Irvine, reported that about 350 Mouache Utes were located at that agency. The settlers located in the area had complained about the travels of the Utes to and from the Colorado reservation and asked that Irvine attempt to have the Utes moved from the area. Irvine pointed out that the agency buildings were located on leased land not permanently owned by the government. The original intent had been only to use the buildings for a short time before making other arrangements for the Utes. Now the settlers were asking him to see that those arrangements were made. In his report to the Commissioner of Indian Affairs, Irvine agreed with the desire of the settlers.

The other agent, S. A. Russell, who was seeing to the needs of the Utes at Abiquiu, agreed with Irvine. He felt these Utes should also be moved from northern New Mexico to southwestern Colorado.

Two years lapsed before Congress acted on the request of the New Mexicans to have the Utes removed to Colorado. The Cimarron agency was ordered closed in 1876, but the Utes had refused to leave the area. Until a solution could be worked out, the government farmer was left to oversee the needs of the Utes. The solution came as part of the appropriations act of 1877. An amendment was added to the bill which stated that the provisions of the 1874 agreement would be carried out and an agency for the Southern Utes located on the southern portion of the reservation.

In May, 1877, Indian agents, Francis A. Weaver and Benjamin M. Thomas, selected a permanent site for the new agency on the Rio de los Pinos, the Pine River, pursuant to provisions of the Indian Appropriations Act of March 3, 1877. By the end of the year, however, the agency had not been built nor had the Indians been removed. Further legislation was necessary before the building and the removal took place. In 1878, that legislation passed Congress, directing the removal of the Utes from New Mexico and the Utes at both Cimarron and Abiquiu were readied for the removal. Some were reluctant and waited hoping that the government would relent. More time was lost waiting for an escort of troops which never arrived. At last, Agent Thomas and Inspector Watkins moved the Utes out of New Mexico in July, 1878. The trip from northern New Mexico took one month. By August 16, 1878, they were located at the site of the new agency. After nearly twenty years' effort the Government had finally moved all of the Utes in New Mexico to one reservation in Colorado.

The Anglos of northern New Mexico were satisfied with the removal of the Utes from their area, but the people of Colorado were not. The gold discovered in the San Juan Cession had brought increased numbers of people to the area. They felt the removal of the Utes into southwestern Colorado would only cause them more problems. Also, Colorado had

57

become a state in 1876, and the Anglo citizens felt that additional Indians would discourage settlers from coming to the state. The citizens called for the complete ouster of the Indians from the state.

As the Utes were being removed from Cimarron and Abiquiu, New Mexico, a commission was being sent to meet with the Utes in negotiations for removal from Colorado. A bill had passed both houses of Congress during the spring of 1878 directing President Rutherford B. Hayes to seek approval from the Colorado Indians for removal. This committee met with the Southern Utes at the same time those Indians from New Mexico were arriving at the Los Pinos Agency.

The commission asked the Southern Utes to move to the northern portion of the Colorado reservation. The Indians refused. Those Utes who had just arrived did not want to move again and the rest refused to live with the northern bands. The Southern Utes did agree, however, to move to a smaller reservation located just north and east of their present reservation at the headwaters of the Piedra, San Juan, and Navajo Rivers.

In exchange for the new reservation, which consisted of 728,320 acres, the Utes were to cede title of their old reservation, nearly 1,894,400 acres, to the government. Compensation was to be given for 1,100,000 acres relinquished and a new agency was to be established on the Navajo River.

Congress wanted the Southern Utes moved onto one common reservation with the Northern bands.

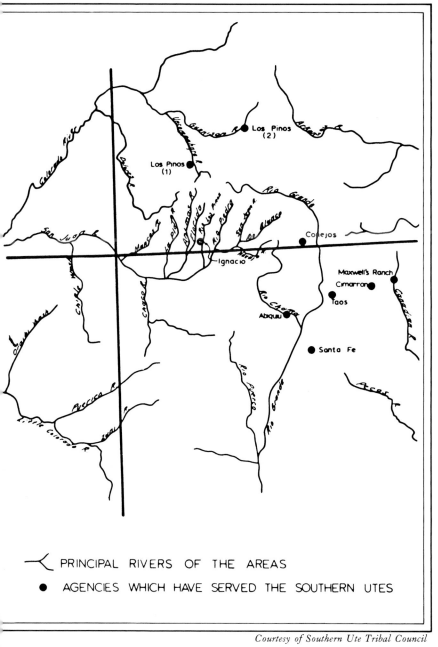

Los Pinos (2)

Los Pinos (1)

Colorado River

San Juan R

Cascade

Piedra R

Mancos R

Rio Piedra

Rio Pine

Rio La Pine

Rio Los Pinos

Rio Blanco

Santa Ana

Rio Grande

Conejos

Ignacio

Maxwell's Ranch

Cimarron

Taos

Rio Chama

Abiquiú

Santa Fe

Rio Pecos

Rio Grande

Canadian R

Arcas

Puerca R

Little Colorado R

Chama

Chama R

Navajo R

San Juan R

Animas R

Arkansas R

⟨ PRINCIPAL RIVERS OF THE AREAS

● AGENCIES WHICH HAVE SERVED THE SOUTHERN UTES

Courtesy of Southern Ute Tribal Council

MAP 3. Principal Rivers.

When the signed agreement from the Southern Utes was presented for approval, Congress refused to grant it. The Colorado delegation was dissatisfied with the compromise and had pressured Congress to seek another solution.

In September, 1879, an incident occurred which focused national attention on the Ute situation and generated public support for Ute removal from Colorado. At the northern agency in White River, the agent, Nathan Meeker, attempted to have the grazing land near the agency plowed in grain. The Indians did not want the good grazing land plowed and they protested. The agent refused to heed their protests and, over-reacting, asked that the army send troops to the agency. The entry of the troops to the reservation caused considerable anger among the Utes. About twenty-five Utes, led by Douglas, attacked the agency, killing Meeker and eight young men working for him. In addition three women and two children were taken captive and held hostage for twenty-three days. At the same time the troops called to the reservation by Meeker were attacked. Nearly three hundred Utes under the leadership of Captain Jack ambushed the soldiers and pinned them down for six days before relief could reach them. These events created a national uproar against the Utes, and the public called for their removal to Indian territory.

Congress instructed the executive branch of the government to negotiate with the Utes for their removal from Colorado. On January 16, 1880,

Ignacio, Buckskin Charlie, Severo and Blanco (Ojo Blanco) representing the Southern Utes, and Ouray and other leaders of the Northern Utes left the reservation for Washington, D.C., to negotiate with officials of the Bureau of Indian Affairs. The Ute leaders agreed to relocate. The agreement signed by them on March 6 was approved by Congress.

In addition to relocating the Utes, the agreement stated that all claim to their reservation would be relinquished. For this they would receive allotments of land along the La Plata River. To seek the approval of the tribal members, a committee of five was to be named by President Hayes. If the agreement was ratified by the tribe, Congress was to give final approval.

The commission named for the tribal negotiations included George W. Manypenny, Alfred B. Meacham, John B. Bowman, John J. Russell, and Otto Mears. After gathering in Denver, Colorado, on June 28, the commission left for the Ute agencies. The negotiations began on August 15, and by September 20, 581 Southern Utes had ratified the agreement. Shortly afterwards the other Ute bands in Colorado followed the Southern Ute example. By December the agreement had been approved.

Immediately the Ute commission began preparation to move the northern bands to the Uintah Reservation in Utah. After a short delay the White River Utes were moved and about one year later the Uncompahgre band was relocated.

Removal of the three Southern Ute bands did not

Photograph Courtesy the Smithsonian Institution, Bureau of American Ethnology

RTRAIT OF SOUTHERN UTE CHIEF IGNACIO taken in 1899.

proceed as the commission had hoped. The lands designated as the new reservation were poor for agriculture and incapable of supporting the Utes. At the same time the Denver and Rio Grande Railroad had reached Durango and was pushing its way up the Animas River to Silverton. The railroad brought more people to the area who again pressured the Utes for their lands. Once more the Utes were caught between the forces of the civilization process. A new reservation had been established for the Indians, but was declared unsuitable for farming, the occupation the BIA hoped the Indians would embrace. The land hungry Anglos wanted not only the lands of the old reservation but the lands of the proposed reservation.

Although the citizens of Colorado pressured Congress for a decision on this dilemma, a solution was not found for a number of years. Two alternatives were presented but each was turned down. One was to move the Colorado Utes onto the Ute reservations in eastern Utah, but the other bands did not want the Southern Utes relocated there and the Southern Utes did not want to move. The second alternative was a suggestion by the Commissioner of Indian Affairs, J. D. C. Atkins, to move the Indians to San Juan County, Utah. Bills were introduced into Congress in 1886 and 1887 asking for this removal but they failed to win support.

In 1888, the removal bill again failed to pass either the House or the Senate. Then Commissioner Atkins added a clause embodying the proposed removal to a bill making an agreement with a group of

Montana Indians. On May 1, 1888, the Montana Indian agreement with the Ute removal clause passed Congress and was signed by the President.

On August 4, a commission of three, J. Montgomery Smith, Thomas S. Childs, and R. D. Weaver, met with the Southern Ute bands at Ignacio. The negotiations took several months before three-fourths of the male population of the three bands agreed to relocate. By January, 1889, the agreement had been sent to Congress for its approval. Within one month the Senate had voted favorably for removal, but the House rejected the agreement.

Those groups against removing the Utes from Colorado who applied enough pressure on the members of the House to vote down the bill included the citizens of Utah, who decided they had too many Indians in their territory already, the Indian Rights Association, a reform group located in Philadelphia who thought progress in civilizing the Utes would be destroyed because of increased isolation from whites, and the cattle companies which used the La Sal and Abajo mountains as grazing areas.

The combined resistance of these groups against removal managed to defeat all removal bills introduced into Congress for the next five years. With each session of Congress, bills were announced that would relocate the Utes in San Juan County, Utah, but all failed. Not until 1894 was a bill presented that received the support of these groups.

The 1895 Bill introduced into Congress by Andrew J. Hunter from Illinois asked that the Utes be located on their old reservation in southwestern Colorado. Individual allotments of land were to be distributed to the Ute families and when all of the families had been given land, then the special status of the reservation was to be removed and the land not taken by the Utes was to be opened to white settlement. The Government hoped that once the Utes had been given the individual allotments that they would become farmers and cultivate the land given to them. The Hunter Act, after some delay in the Senate, passed both Houses of Congress and was signed into law by President Grover Cleveland on February 11, 1895.

Before the bill could be implemented, the Utes had to agree to it. A commission consisting of Meredith H. Kidd, Thomas P. Smith, Assistant Commissioner of Indian Affairs, and David F. Day, Southern Ute Agent, was sent to the reservation to explain the new bill to the Southern Utes and to gain their approval. Within several months 153 of the 301 eligible male adult Utes primarily from the Mouaches and Capote bands had signed the new agreement. The margin of difference between those wanting to remain on the old reservation and those wanting to move to a new location was only five votes. The Secretary of Interior decided, however, that the Southern Utes wanted the new agreement and approved the five vote margin.

When the Utes approved the agreement, a new commission was named to distribute the allotments. By April, 1896, 72,811 acres of land had been allotted to 371 Utes, generally on the basis of 160 acres for each head of the household with one-half share, or eighty acres, allotted to orphans, single adults, and other special cases. The Department of Indian Affairs approved these allotments on June 12.

Because one-half of the Southern Utes voted against the 1894 agreement and the planned allotments, the Government officials felt obliged to accommodate them. Those Utes against the agreement included almost the entire Weeminuche band under the leadership of Ignacio. Earlier they had wanted to move to San Juan County, Utah, and had moved there when the 1888 agreement had been approved by the tribe. Later when the agreement had failed to pass Congress the Southern Ute Agency had been forced to bring them back to Colorado. They refused to return to the Los Pinos agency, however, and established a camp on the western end of the old Southern Ute Reservation, which was retained as land-in-common for Ignacio and his band while those areas of the eastern end not taken by the allotments were opened for Anglo settlement. A sub-agency was opened for the Weeminuche at Navajo Springs in 1897. This was the beginning of the separation of the three bands of the Southern Utes into two groups, the Mouache and Capote bands located on the eastern portion of the former reservation and the Weeminuche band located on the western end of the reservation. After the turn of the century the two sections became known as the Ute Mountain Reservation, the home of the

Severo.

JDIO PORTRAIT of Southern Ute Chief Severo.

Weeminuche band, and the Southern Ute Reservation, the home of the Mouache and Capote bands.

Once the allotments were given to the Capotes and the Mouaches and the reservation established for the Weeminuches, the remaining lands, 523,079 acres, of the old reservation were ready for Anglo settlement at a minimum of $1.25 per acre. On May 4, 1899, President William McKinley signed the proclamation and the reservation was opened. This act marked the end of another era in Southern Ute history.

THE TWENTIETH CENTURY: ADAPTATION

The first years of the twentieth century were not kind to the Capote and Mouache Utes. Their old life style was gone and they found it exceedingly difficult to make a living by farming. They did only what they had to do to keep meagre crops alive, working only as long as great need existed and apparently believing that the federal government would take care of them if they failed. Some of the Southern Utes preferred to live with their kin than move to their own allotted lands and farm them. This gave rise to a general opinion among non-Indians of the surrounding area that all Utes were lazy.

In 1900, rations were being issued on a semimonthly basis at a *per capita* cost of $13. Each head of household was issued an amount proportionate to the size of his family living at home. One and one-half pounds of beef or bacon and one-half pound of flour was the ordinary daily maximum

71

with four pounds of coffee, three pounds of beans, and seven pounds of sugar distributed to every 100 rations. This rationing system was not a "something-for-nothing" proposition. Congress in 1875 required that all able bodied males between eighteen and forty-five years of age provide services beneficial to the tribe in an amount equal to the rations received.

Gradually, members of the two bands adapted to the new way of life. By 1915, they had made great advances in farming their lands. A total of over 2000 acres were planted in alfalfa, wheat, oats, beans, and potatoes. In that year alone, 700 acres had been cleared and cultivated and thirty-two more had started to farm their allotments. Farm machinery was provided at prices below wholesale, e.g., McCormick Mowing Machines at $45, Binders at $100, Studebaker 3-inch wagons at $65, galvanized barbed wire at $2.50 per 100 lbs. Forty-eight horses were bought for those Indians at a cost of $75-$100 per head and twenty-four sets of harness were purchased so that those horses could be used. The government also made an attempt to bring the Southern Utes closer to the agency at Ignacio by arranging transfers of land between Indians and non-Indians and by purchasing tracts of good land closer to Ignacio. It was the opinion of the Commissioner of Indian Affairs in 1915:

> If the present policy of dealing with the Utes is continued, in a few years this valley [Pine River] will be hard to recognize as the same country . . . We can now

look forward to the time when we will point with pride to the many well-kept farms of our Ute neighbors and when we will be able to consider these people as citizens and assets to our community.

Of course, such good reports did not apply to all members. Rations and per capita payments continued to be made in accordance with stipulations of the Agreement of 1880 ". . . a sum of money or its equivalent in bonds of the United States, which shall be sufficient to produce the sum of $50,000 per annum, which sum of $50,000 shall be distributed per capita to them forever." Between 1919 and 1929, Southern Ute families received an average of $613.20 per year. Rationing was finally discontinued in 1931, although Commissioner Seymour had recommended in 1923:

> . . . these Utes are making substantial progress in industry. Good harvests and provision for the needs of the coming winter are everywhere in evidence. From an economic point of view the situation seemed a satisfactory one. I regret to see the issue of rations continued to a people to whom it is no longer a necessity. I recommend the elimination of the ration roll as soon as it can be done conformably to treaty obligations.

Toward the end of the third decade of the twentieth century, the Mouaches and Capotes began to raise sheep. The Agreement of 1895 stated that, after unallotted lands were sold at a minimum of $1.25 per acre, certain amounts of the proceeds were to be invested in sheep. This provision had not been acted upon until Mr. Dickens, superintendent of the Consolidated Ute Agency, persuaded the Utes to accept it

73

and bought for them five head for each man, woman, and child. By 1932, the flocks had grown considerably and they were allowed to graze on forest reserve land at a nominal cost per head. Wool was sold to a buyer in Boston for a price higher than non-Indians were getting. Strangely, at that time, only three families owned cattle to a total number of 120 head, although there had been many more cattle in earlier times. Almost every family had chickens but none kept hogs. Some supplemented their agricultural income by wage-work pursuits but the transition was not an easy one largely because of the poor nature of the land. The annual average precipitation of sixteen to twenty-two inches supports only the native vegetation of sage, oakbrush, piñon pine, juniper, and various range grasses. The Utes had to learn the techniques of irrigation as a means of raising food and forage crops.

During this period of difficult adjustment to an agricultural economy, the Southern Utes were fortunate to have Buckskin Charlie as Chief. He had been named Chief at the request of Ouray, when that great leader was dying in 1880. There was not a voice to dissent from Ouray's plea. Ouray had named Charlie as leader of the Mouache band about 1870 and he served as a sub-chief under Ouray and had learned from him a great deal about dealing with people. In 1880, Buckskin Charlie was forty years old. He and Severo were the principal leaders of the Capotes and Mouaches. Severo died in 1913 and Charlie continued as principal chief of both bands.

74

He had had a great many experiences from the time that he had been born to a Ute father and an Apache mother. He had served as an army scout, had gone to Washington with Ouray in 1880 and, in 1905, with a band of 350 Utes he had marched in the inaugural parade of Theodore Roosevelt.

Even before land was allotted to individual Utes, Buckskin Charlie lived in the Pine River valley and grew crops for his family and his livestock. At the time of allotment, he received the land upon which he had been living. He was the principal influence in the change from food gathering and hunting to agricultural pursuits. His advice was sought and listened to with respect and he was trusted and admired by Indian and non-Indian alike. He could speak English but preferred his native Ute tongue. When he visited with non-Indians, he wore white man's clothes but he insisted that all traditional tribal festivals and ceremonies be held in the old ways and he encouraged the continuation of the old arts and crafts. Charlie was always seeking new and better ways to farm, as a means of enhancing the livelihood of his people. Chief Buckskin Charlie died in May, 1936, and was buried near his old friend, Ouray. Another era had passed.

THE TWENTIETH CENTURY: PROGRESS

Under terms of the Wheeler-Howard (Indian Reorganization) Act of June, 1934, the Capote and Mouache bands officially adopted the name, Southern Ute Tribe. Also, the intent of that Act was to

SOUTHERN UTE CHIEF BUCKSKIN CHARLIE in center wearing a United States Pea

Photograph Courtesy the Smithsonian Institution, Bureau of American Ethnology

dallion.

provide self-government and a greater degree of Indian management of his own resources and responsibility for his own destiny. The Act halted further allotments of land to individual Indians, limited the sale of land of deceased Indians except to the tribe, and returned any surplus lands to Indian ownership. The emphasis was to be on the tribe or group rather than on the individual. Accordingly, the Southern Utes drew up a Constitution and By-laws which was ratified on November 4, 1936, and provided for a chairman and a council of six members to conduct tribal affairs. Antonio Buck, Sr., the son of Buckskin Charlie, was elected to be the first chairman of the Tribal Council and served from 1936 to 1939, and as respected elder statesman of the tribe until his death in 1961. In 1937, 222,016 acres of land were returned to the Southern Utes by virtue of the Restoration Act.

Tony Buck sustained the program of agricultural advancement sponsored by his father, but the Southern Utes suffered from the Great Depression along with all their fellow Americans. Some of them lived in abject poverty but eked out an existence on their farm or by wage labor sponsored by projects of the federal government. One such project, supervised by the Works Progress Administration, created a memorial to four great leaders: Ouray, Severo, Ignacio, and Buckskin Charlie. It still draws visitors to Ute Memorial Park, close to the newly constructed tourist complex. The annual per capita income of the Southern Utes in 1939 was only $187.

Despite the poverty level of the 1930's, Southern Utes continued their ranching and farming enterprises to the point where their lambs, wool, beef, and grain contributed to the war effort of the 1940's. The war economy, too, contributed to higher prices for their products and for their labor. In addition, over eighty young men of the tribe served in the armed forces. The return of these veterans at the end of World War II brought new knowledge and new insights into the tribe which would presage a new era and new leadership for the future.

Experience throughout the 40's and 50's in determining their own programs and in being responsible for their own destiny brought confidence to members of the tribe. They found that the Tribal Council was interested in representing all segments of the membership and that the Tribal Chairman was approachable to listen to complaints and suggestions. The first Tribal Chairman, Antonio Buck, steered the group into democratic self-government during his term, 1936 to 1939. He was succeeded by Julius Cloud, who held the office of Tribal Chairman for the long period from 1939 to 1948. Sam Burch then served in that capacity from 1948 to 1950 to be succeeded by Julius Cloud again from 1950 to 1952. Sam Burch served the next four years, 1952-1956. His successor was John E. Baker, Sr., who had been asked by tribal officials to leave college to prepare the Rehabilitation Plan presented later in this book. Mr. Baker served as Tribal Chairman from 1956 to 1960 and again from 1961 to 1962, with Anthony Burch filling the position for the intervening year. John S. Williams was Chairman from 1962 to 1965. He was succeeded by Leonard C. Burch, Anthony's younger brother, who has held the position from 1966 to the present time.

During the first half of the twentieth century, the Southern Utes lost a great deal of their cultural heritage as they were trying to adjust to a whole new way of life. Perhaps, this is best illustrated by the fact that when live cattle were issued as part of the rations, men of the tribe would let the cattle out of a corral, chase and kill them as they had been accustomed to killing game in the old days. During this time, too, their old arts and crafts were almost forgotten.

On the other hand, there has been a renaissance among the Southern Utes in recent years. Apparently, they have decided to keep the best of the new ways and all of the old ways considered necessary to their identity as individuals and Southern Utes. In the spring time, the Bear Dance is a general tribal festival celebrated with prayers, songs, and dancing in which they are usually joined by their Ute relatives, the Northern Utes and the Ute Mountain Utes plus other Indians from the surrounding region. The Sun Dance is celebrated in the summer and draws many visitors to the reservation. Generally, the Utes are quite religious practicing their ancient rites or participating in several denominations of the Christian religion. Beadwork and other crafts are being practiced again and the visitor will find some for sale in the new Tourist Center.

No reading can claim to give an exact knowledge of a people. Flesh and blood are rarely projected onto the pages of a book. The person interested in the Southern Utes should spend some time with them and get to know them on an individual basis. It will be an unforgettable and rewarding experience for young and old alike. Persons who do make a visit will understand what the Southern Utes are trying to accomplish and the obstacles involved in learning to compete in a very technological environment within a very few decades. That person who is truly interested in the Southern Utes will probably want to keep abreast of developments by subscribing to *The Southern Ute Drum*, the newspaper published by the tribe.

THE FUTURE

Perhaps, the basis for the future of the Southern Utes was laid when, on July 13, 1950, the United States Court of Claims adjudged that land had been taken illegally from the Utes from 1891 to 1938 and that, therefore, the Confederated Bands of Ute Indians were entitled to $31,761,207.62. Public Law 120 directed the Secretary of the Interior "to divide the trust funds belonging to the Confederated Bands of Ute Indians . . . by crediting sixty per cent to the Ute Indian Tribe of the Uintah and Ouray Reservation, consisting of the Uintah, Uncompahgre, and White River Utes, and forty per cent to the Southern

Utes, consisting of the Southern Utes of the Southern Ute Reservation and the Ute Mountain Tribe of the Ute Mountain Reservation". Thus, the share of the Southern Utes amounted to approximately six million dollars.

In the early spring of 1951, the Albuquerque Area Office of the Bureau of Indian Affairs instructed the Southern Ute Tribal Council to draw up plans for the use of their share of the money. This was one of the first instances in which these Indians had been told that they could make their own plans. The Utes took entire responsibility for their plans to determine the best use of the new resources and received from the Bureau of Indian Affairs only such assistance as was requested. The primary goal was an early withdrawal from dependence on the BIA, so the Southern Ute people could function as a normal American community. Progress reports were to be provided by the Agency superintendent to the BIA if they were requested, regarding projected use of the money.

It was decided that an initial amount should be large enough to make a practical social and economic difference in the living standard of every household. This payment should be sufficient to build a house, to invest in cattle or sheep, to buy farm machinery, to have wells and sanitary facilities installed in homes, or to provide a college education for the young members of the family. In short, the sum was to be large enough for short range improvement, but not large enough to jeopardize a long range plan of betterment.

Although there was some dissent from members of the Tribe who believed that the immediate per capita payment should be larger, this plan largely prevailed and demonstrated that, indeed, the Southern Utes were ready for complete self-government and the determination of their own future.

Planning continued and the Southern Utes decided, in 1956, that their desires were embodied in fourteen goals, which were presented to the Commissioner of Indian Affairs in that year. These goals are as follows:

1. The attainment of a constructive family community life through sound social practices.

2. That the Southern Ute children will receive the advantages of non-segregated public school education.

That a sufficient number of high school graduates will complete a college education in order to supply needed Southern Ute leadership qualified in technical and professional fields, and to secure professional employment off the Reservation. That a sufficient number of Southern Utes will be trained in the skilled trades to meet Reservation and off-reservation employment needs.

3. That through modern sanitation and the use of the best available medical services the average health standard of the Southern Ute people will equal or exceed the non-Indian standards.

4. The establishment of a sound credit service, operated in compliance with accepted credit procedures, which will be large enough to meet the justifi-

able needs of the Southern Ute people off and on reservation and that this credit facility will be controlled by the Southern Utes.

5. That, that part of the Southern Ute Land Code relating to assigned lands will be so revised as to provide equitable protection to the Tribe and so those people may thus feel justified and secure in building homes and providing these lands. That this revised code will also provide for more equitable distribution of the benefits of these lands to all Southern Utes.

6. That the living conditions of the Southern Ute people will be improved through better housing, modern sanitation, the drilling of domestic water wells, electrical power and equipment, telephones and modern home management.

7. That agricultural production on Southern Ute farms will be increased through the coordinated efforts of the Indian farmer, the Indian Service personnel and outside agricultural agencies.

8. That 4000 acres of irrigable land be developed by subjugating virgin land now under canal on the Pine River Project.

9. That livestock production will be increased through better range management and improvement practices developed by trained Southern Ute stockmen.

10. That a timber management plan sponsored by the Southern Ute Tribe will increase timber revenues on a sustained-yield basis.

11. That the BIA will complete an all-weather road system on the Southern Ute Reservation, sub-

ject to availability of funds. This is basic to the entire Rehabilitation Program.

12. That all-weather access roads to farmsteads be constructed and financed when necessary by long-term loans to Ute farmers.

13. That the opportunities for Southern Ute operated private enterprises shall be expanded.

14. That Southern Ute officials and people will participate more actively in the management of the business involving tribal resources.

To carry out these goals, it was necessary to create organizations within the tribal structure. New departments began to place social and economic developments on a sound basis.

The Tribal Credit Fund launched in 1956 administers the tribal credit fund program, handling loan approvals and operational plans.

Office of the Program Director, created in 1954, serves as the business management end of the Tribe. This office keeps employment records and job opportunities, counsels and supervises several groups, and initiates and develops management procedures, among other functions.

The Business Office, also established in 1954, maintains tribal financial records, and receives and disburses funds.

The Agricultural Resources Committee, another 1954 innovation, is an advisory body to the Tribal Council. Its purpose concerns land use and exchange and general agricultural matters.

In 1955, the Land Operations Office was established to work out agricultural problems between farmers on the reservation and Indian Service workers. Later, the Agricultural Resources Enterprise plan was set up. This plan had $62,800 appropriated for equipment and $20,000 for operating expenses. Its purpose was to help farmers clear and level land, build fences, ditches, and farm reservoirs, seed land, spray for weed control, fertilize, and prevent erosion. If a farmer needed help, he applied for it and was charged only for the actual work value. This plan created new jobs for the tribe, gave Utes the experience of operating heavy equipment, and most important, helped the farmers in the area.

A farmer may have had 200 acres, for instance, but fifty of those acres may not have been suitable for the plow. To be an economical unit, that is, 175 acres of arable land for a farming enterprise, or sufficient land to feed 100 head of cattle or 500 head of sheep, at least twenty-five acres of this person's land had to be cleared. This was a goal of the Agricultural Resources Enterprise plan. As of 1958, thirteen farmers had economical units as compared with four in 1956.

The timber management plan as outlined in Goal #10 had to be modified in 1958 because of low profits from poor conditions. The new plan called for cutting timber in large quantities every few years up through 1964 and then letting the forests "rest" for ten years. This plan was to give the Tribe a net return of $80,000+ per year, as opposed to the $18,000 of the first plan.

As the first years of the Rehabilitation Plan drew to a close, many of the original fourteen goals were well under way, not only in the area of economics but also in education, health, credit, roads and general well-being of the family and community life.

During the first half of the 1960's, several other departments were organized for economic purposes.

The Fish and Game program sells tribal hunting and fishing licenses and keeps tabs on fish and game offenders. In its first years, the department offered a $20.00 permit for a three-animal limit if the hunter had a state game license. Later the permit was raised to $40.00 and the maximum reduced to two animals. Fishing rights on the rivers running through the reservation were hard to determine because of the checkerboarding. The sale of these licenses was not as great as that of the game permits.

The Office of the Treasurer signs and distributes all tribal checks and is responsible for all checks made by the tribal business office.

From the years 1960-1965 the volume and gross return from timber nearly doubled. The tribe grossed $82,141 in the final year of the study. Christmas tree and post permits rose from $150 in 1960 to $716 in 1965.

Gas income has been a great source of income for the Southern Ute people. A pipeline supplying natural gas to Gunnison and Climax, among other towns, was completed in 1963. The Western Slope Gas Company, which operates the above, also paid $13,837.38 for a right-of-way over Southern Ute

Photograph by John I. Griffin

IS BUILDING WAS ORIGINALLY CONSTRUCTED by the United States Government to
✓e as the school for Indian children. Today it contains the offices for the Tribe's
adstart Program and their Day Care Center. A picturesque part of the Southern Ute's
bal Government complex.

lands. The company estimates that gas from the reservation will be profitable for at least thirty years.

Gas, oil, and grazing leases are important to the Ute. Of the tribal lands, 159,509.74 acres are under gas and oil leases, and 31,980.89 acres are leased for grazing and agriculture. Of the allotted lands, 4,118 acres make up gas and oil leases, and 4,035.92 are under agricultural and grazing leases. These figures were current as of 1965.

Per capita income in 1960 was about $900. The payments from 1960-64 were to be reduced $100 annually by a proposal of the Tribal Council.

During the 1970's, great strides have been and will continue to be taken in economic development. In the twenty years since the beginnings of the Rehabilitation Plan of the Southern Utes, the tribe has pulled itself up by its bootstraps and is making progress every day.

Timber resources are important avenues of income to the tribe. The ponderosa pine forests still have much potential. There is a great amount of timber to be cut yet of these 30,000 acres classed as commercial forest lands. These forests will be left to rest for thirty or forty years; the next harvest program will begin in 2000 A.D.

So far the only uses for piñon pine and juniper have been for fence posts and fuel. Possibly in the future there could be much demand for these types of timber, and about 122,000 acres remain.

The following table shows the volume of remaining timber species, out of 152,528 acres:

Ponderosa pine	99,483,000 bd. ft.
Douglas fir	7,980,000 bd. ft.
White fir	3,133,000 bd. ft.
Piñon pine	27,665,000 bd. ft.
Juniper	2,661,000 bd. ft.

According to a 1964 report, over 50,000 acres of gas and oil potential were estimated. Coal beds indicate an abundance of the substance — 300 million tons. In the same year, 1964, a two-year exploration project covering 98,250 acres was undertaken by the Peabody Coal Company. A 1973 report presenting an analysis of reservation minerals is not available at this time. Sand and gravel operations and clay beds could be developed but it is not known whether these would be feasible and/or profitable.

Lake Capote, near Chimney Rock, has great potential. As of now, there is a public campground with running water adjacent to the lake. Lake Capote is a well-stocked lake of fifty-two acres. Its potential has not been realized due to the remote entrance to the area. Improvements of this project, due to increased tourism on the reservation, will be discussed below.

During the past ten years, out-of-state hunters have made use of the reservation for excellent hunting. It is a relatively safe area in which to hunt deer, elk, turkey, and bear.

The Southern Ute Community Center and Pino Nuche Motel were opened in January, 1972. The motel has enjoyed a high rate of occupancy of its thirty-eight rooms. Several large conventions have

Photograph by Robert Delaney

NO NUCHE PU-RÁ-SA from a near-by mesa.

requested accommodations, but the motel has had to turn them down. Plans are in the making for the expansion of the motel by 100 rooms to accommodate these large groups. In this complex are also located a restaurant, museum, and arts and crafts shop, along with some tribal offices. By 1975, a paved road is planned between Ignacio and Dulce, New Mexico, the headquarters of the Jicarilla Apaches, to create a link with that new tourist development.

The goal of giving private enterprise the opportunity to expand, as outlined previously, has not been realized. Only a few individuals were engaged in businesses. Plans for a shopping center are being developed. The businesses to be included in this complex are a convenience store, beauty and barber shops, self-service laundry and dry-cleaning, along with a commercial laundry service, an auto service station, variety store, TV and appliance repair, bank, sporting goods store, snack and sandwich shops, and a drug store, which will have a pharmacist.

Other plans are for a tribally-owned horse training and conditioning center. Apparently the altitude at the Southern Ute Reservation is ideal for this type of enterprise. The present fairgrounds will be used. Additional buildings such as barns with individual stalls for horses, and feed storage areas, along with areas for conditioning the horses will be built. This project would provide income for tribal members who will be trained professionally to handle the horses. About twenty-five members will be employed, and approval was given in February, 1974, for a $668,000 grant to begin this project.

Southwestern Colorado, because of its climate and relative isolation, has become one of the most popular tourist areas in the West. The Southern Ute Reservation is located in close proximity to Mesa Verde National Park, the Durango-Silverton narrow gauge train, and excellent outdoor recreation areas. Several projects are being planned to divert at least some of this heavy tourist traffic, possibly even to make the reservation a focal point rather than an afternoon side trip from nearby attractions.

An historical Indian village will be located opposite the tourist center on Highway 172, the main artery to Ignacio. This village will have authentic dwellings and life-styles of the Southern Utes from pre-historic times to modern living. It is planned to be life-size to permit visitors to walk through and really get the feeling of the Ute way of living, and Indian foods gathered from the area such as wild honey, choke-cherry products, and piñon nuts will be sold.

The Southern Ute Memorial Chapel will be open to visitors on a limited basis, permitting them to see the spiritual side of the Southern Utes. This chapel will be constructed of native materials wherever possible.

An outdoor recreation complex will include a picnic and playground area, baseball diamonds, concession stands, bleachers and outdoor lighting for Indian ceremonials, dances, and games.

A camper-trailer park on the Pine River, east of the tourist center, will have fifty trailer spaces and sanitary facilities. Modern vacationers are accustomed to this type of "camping out" and this will fulfill their needs.

The swimming pool at the tourist complex will be enclosed to provide an additional attraction during the winter months for visitors to the center.

A bowling alley, ice skating rink, Olympic-size swimming pool, and bicycle and backpacking areas will be constructed, to the benefit of both the community and to the public.

As stated before, the Lake Capote recreational area has not reached its full potential. An entrance directly from Highway 160 is to be provided. Other plans include a commercial campground, grocery and gift stores, gas station, snack bar, and swimming pool. Lake Capote may possibly be enlarged.

Since Lake Capote and Chimney Rock are in close proximity, hiking trails may be constructed from one to the other. About six miles of these trails are to be completed. The Chimney Rock Archaeological Site may become an attraction for this area as Mesa Verde is for the Durango-Cortez area.

A present-day Indian village proposed would be a living model of Southern Ute life during the tourist season. Tours could be taken and ceremonials held for the public.

The planned Southern Ute Fine Arts Center will be located adjacent to the historical village already mentioned. The present museum and arts and crafts shop will be moved to this new location due to a lack of space in the current facilities. The Fine Arts Center would include sound-proof reading and music listening areas, a library, and an art gallery for permanent and travelling art collections. The tribe expects to receive a $17,000 grant soon through the Federal Library Service and Construction Act (Title 1).

Other projects planned are an archery range, par 3 golf course, and a living natural history museum to depict and interpret flora and fauna of the area surrounding Ignacio.

All of the above should not indicate that the future of the Southern Utes is completely unclouded. There remain many problems to be solved such as the need for an increase of employment opportunities, the need for better education, and the need for more tribal unity. The natural resources and especially the human resources of the Southern Utes are great. The Southern Ute people will continue to develop, expand, and improve. They have marched a long way since filtering into the Rockies but the remaining few years of the twentieth century may well witness more changes and developments than the last eight or nine centuries. There are several cases in United States courts regarding the adjudication of water rights for the Southern Utes. It is my fervent hope that these cases come out successfully for the Southern Utes thus enabling them to develop their reservation to a much greater extent for the benefit of all the Tribal members.

98

For the person interested in researching Ute history, two bibliographies are essential:

STEWART, OMER C., *Ethnohistorical Bibliography of the Ute Indians of Colorado*. University of Colorado Studies: Series in Anthropology, No. 18, Boulder, University of Colorado Press, 1971.

TYLER, S. LYMAN, *The Ute People: A Bibliographical Checklist*. Provo, Brigham Young University, 1964.

Spanish and Mexican contacts with the Utes have been quite thoroughly researched and presented in several articles. Among the most useful are:

HILL, JOSEPH J., "Spanish and New Mexican Exploration and Trade Northwest from New Mexico into the Great Basin", *Utah Historical Quarterly*, III, 1930.

SCHROEDER, ALBERT H., "A Brief History of the Southern Utes", *Southwestern Lore*, XXX, No. 4, October, 1954.

TYLER, S. LYMAN, "The Spaniard and the Ute", *Utah Historical Quarterly*, XXII, No. 4, October, 1954.

TYLER, S. LYMAN, "The Yuta Indians before 1680", *Western Humanities Review*, V, Spring, 1951.

The records of the Spanish and Mexican governments are kept at the New Mexico State Records Center in Santa Fe, New Mexico. These records have now been microfilmed and have been acquired by many university libraries.

United States relations with the Utes are detailed in numerous documents contained in the *Capital Serial Set*. Documents relating to the Southern Utes alone comprise more than 5,000 pages. Most of these have been collected together into thirty-four bound volumes known as "The Southern Ute Archival Collection." Included are treaties, agreements, administrative letters, scholarly theses and dissertations, maps, and photographs. They are kept in the office of Tribal Chairman, Leonard Burch, at the Tribal Affairs Building, Ignacio, Colorado. It is a unique collection both in size and selectivity unrivaled by the holdings of any other Indian tribe in the United States. Any serious researcher should start here to understand Ute history from the viewpoint of the United States governmental agencies.

Ceremonial and religious aspects of the Southern Utes are best understood by reading the numerous articles and dissertation written by Marvin K. Opler. Exact citations are contained in the two bibliographies mentioned above. Further information on these aspects is contained in James Jefferson, Robert

W. Delaney, and Gregory C. Thompson, *The Southern Utes: A Tribal History*. Southern Ute Tribe, 1972. This book with its bibliography and chronology of Ute history offers a quick review of Ute history to the reader. Two other books on the Southern Utes are worthy of mention: Wilson Rockwell, *The Utes, A Forgotten People*. Denver, Sage Books, 1956 and Robert Emmitt, *The Last War Trail: The Utes and the Settlement of Colorado*. Norman, University of Oklahoma Press, 1954.

Of course, the person interested in the Southern Utes should arrange to spend some time on the reservation. He will be cordially and graciously received and will gain an insight into these people which can never be acquired by reading books and articles.

TRIBAL SEAL of the Southern Ute.

ROBERT W. DELANEY, Professor of History and Southwest Studies, is currently (since 1964) Director of the Center of Southwest Studies at Fort Lewis College, Durango, Colorado. He has also served as Chairman of the Division of Humanities, Chairman of the Department of History, and Director of the School of Arts and Sciences at that institution. Since 1957, he has been especially concerned with the history of the Southern Utes and other tribes of the Southwest and currently teaches a two-semester course on the history of the Indians of New Mexico, Arizona, California, Nevada, Utah, and Colorado. He has lectured widely on this subject and on various aspects of Latin American history. He is the author of several articles in scholarly publications, numerous book reviews, and was co-author of *The Southern Utes, A Tribal History* (1972).